CAMBRIDGE

Official Cambridge Exam Preparation

CB126762

B1 PRELIMINARY 2

WITHOUT ANSWERS

AUTHENTIC PRACTICE TESTS

Cambridge University Press
www.cambridge.org/elt

Cambridge Assessment English
www.cambridgeenglish.org

Information on this title: www.cambridge.org/9781108748759

First published 2020

20 19 18 17 16 15 14 13 12 11 10 9 8 7 6 5 4

Printed in Great Britain by Ashford Colour Press Ltd.

A catalogue record for this publication is available from the British Library

ISBN 978-1-108-78155-8 B1 Preliminary 2 Student's Book with Answers with Audio
ISBN 978-1-108-74875-9 B1 Preliminary 2 Student's Book without Answers

Contents

Introduction

Prepare for the exam with practice tests from Cambridge

Inside you'll find four authentic examination papers from Cambridge Assessment English. They are the perfect way to practise – EXACTLY like the real exam.

Why are they unique?

All our authentic practice tests go through the same design process as the *B1 Preliminary* exam. We check every single part of our practice tests with real students under exam conditions, to make sure we give you the most authentic experience possible.

Students can practise these tests on their own or with the help of a teacher to familiarise themselves with the exam format, understand the scoring system and practise exam technique.

Cambridge English Qualifications	**CEFR Level**	**UK National Qualifications Framework Level**
C2 Proficiency	C2	3
C1 Advanced	C1	2
B2 First	B2	1
B1 Preliminary	B1	Entry 3
A2 Key	A2	Entry 2

Further information

The information contained in this practice book is designed to be an overview of the exam. For a full description of all of the above exams, including information about task types, testing focus and preparation, please see the relevant handbooks, which can be obtained from the Cambridge Assessment English website at: **cambridgeenglish.org**.

The structure of *B1 Preliminary*: an overview

The *Cambridge English Qualifications B1 Preliminary* examination consists of four papers:

Reading: 45 minutes
Candidates need to be able to understand the main points from signs, newspapers and magazines and use vocabulary and structures correctly.

Writing: 45 minutes
Candidates need to be able to respond to an email and to write either an article or a story.

Listening: 30 minutes approximately (plus 6 minutes to transfer answers)
Candidates need to show they can follow and understand a range of spoken materials including announcements and discussions about everyday life.

Speaking: 10–12 minutes (or 15–17 minutes for groups of 3)
Candidates take the Speaking test with another candidate or in a group of three. They are tested on their ability to take part in different types of interaction: with the examiner, with the other candidate and by themselves.

	Overall length	Number of tasks/parts	Number of items
Reading	45 mins	6	32
Writing	45 mins	2	–
Listening	approx. 30 mins	4	25
Speaking	10–12 mins	4	–
Total	approx. 2 hours 10 mins		

Grading

All candidates receive a Statement of Results and candidates whose performance ranges between CEFR Levels A2 and B2 (Cambridge English Scale scores of 120–170) also receive a certificate.

- Candidates who achieve **Grade A** (Cambridge English Scale scores of 160–170) receive the Preliminary English Test certificate stating that they demonstrated ability at Level B2.
- Candidates who achieve **Grade B** or **C** (Cambridge English Scale scores of 140–159) receive the Preliminary English Test certificate at Level B1.
- Candidates whose performance is below B1 level, but falls within **Level A2** (Cambridge English Scale scores of 120–139), receive a Cambridge English certificate stating that they demonstrated ability at Level A2.

For further information on grading and results, go to the website (see page 5 for details).

Speaking: an overview for candidates

The Speaking test lasts 10–12 minutes (or 15–17 minutes for groups of 3). You will take the test with another candidate. There are two examiners but only one of them will talk to you. The examiner will ask you questions and ask you to talk to the other candidate.

Part 1 (2–3 minutes)
The examiner will ask you and your partner some questions in turn. These questions will be about your personal details, daily routines, likes, dislikes, etc. You will only speak to the examiner in this part.

Part 2 (2–3 minutes)
The examiner will give you a colour photograph to talk about. The photograph will show an everyday situation. You will be given one minute to describe what you can see in the photograph.

Part 3 (3–4 minutes)
In this part, you and your partner will talk to each other. The examiner will give you a card with some illustrations on it that are connected to an imaginary situation. You will then be given about two minutes to discuss ideas with your partner. During the discussion, you should make and respond to suggestions, discuss alternatives, make recommendations and negotiate agreement with your partner.

Part 4 (3 minutes)
The examiner will ask you and your partner some questions about the topic introduced in Part 3. The questions will focus on your likes, dislikes, habits and opinions. The examiner will either ask you to respond individually to the questions, or to discuss them with your partner.

Test 1

READING (45 minutes)

Part 1

Questions 1–5

For each question, choose the correct answer.

1

What is Timo worried about?

A The tickets they bought for the match cost too much.

B The weather may be too bad for them to get to the match.

C They could lose the money they spent on tickets.

2

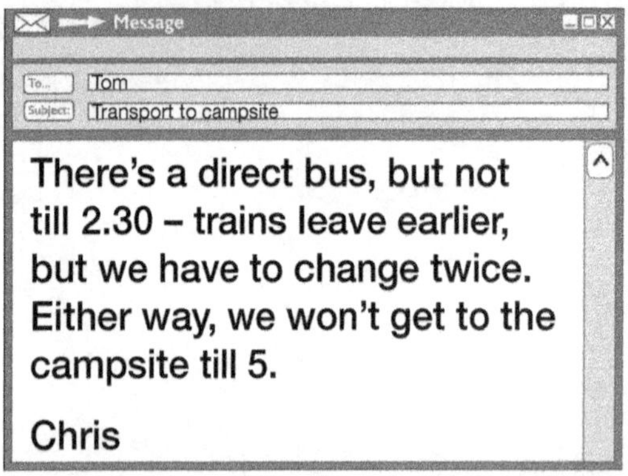

A The journey by bus will take them as long as the one by train.

B They can be on a bus before the first train leaves the station.

C They'll arrive at the same time whether they go by bus or train.

3

Free delivery in 3-5 days on all orders over £30!
Next-day delivery available for extra charge – click here for details

A Anything you order will be delivered within five days for no charge.

B There is a faster delivery option for customers willing to pay more.

C If you spend more than £30 today, items will be delivered for free tomorrow.

4 

A The ingredients on the recipe cards are sold at a discount.

B The supermarket is giving customers ideas for new dishes.

C People can buy interesting meals from the supermarket this week.

5 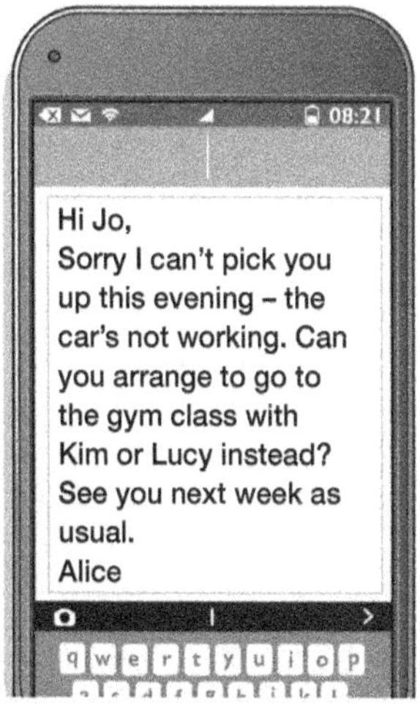

A Jo should contact someone else for a lift tonight.

B Alice can't attend the gym class next week.

C Kim will go to the class with Lucy instead of Jo.

Part 2

Questions 6–10

For each question, choose the correct answer.

The people below are all looking for a music website.
On the opposite page there are eight descriptions of music websites.
Decide which website would be the most suitable for the people below.

6 

Jing wants to find a website that has information on local concerts. She'd like to do online music quizzes and also watch videos which teach you how to play different instruments.

7 

Hans would like to read interviews with musicians and be able to upload videos of his band onto the website. He's also looking for adverts for second-hand guitars.

8 

Precious would like a website where she can find out about piano lessons in her area. She also wants information on music from around the world, and reviews of artists' new recordings.

9 

Antonio wants to read about the history of music and get advice on improving his singing skills. He'd like to find information about shops selling instruments near where he lives.

10 

Nikoleta wants a site that focuses on very old music. She'd also like to learn how to read music, and be able to chat online with music lovers like herself.

The best music websites

A allofusmusic.com

Whether you're a singer in a band or play violin in an orchestra, allofusmusic.com has what you need. If you've filmed your own recordings, why not put them on this website? You can enjoy other people's performances from many international locations, as well as videos of professional concerts.

B musixyes.net

If you're looking for used or new musical equipment and aren't sure where to go, musixyes.net has a list of every store in the country. There are interviews with famous singers and musicians who give tips on becoming as good as they are, and articles on the development of music around the world through the centuries.

C musicisus.com

A great site if you're into singing, especially opera and other traditional music. There are links to different music schools if you're looking for classes, and an excellent collection of step-by-step video guides for learning a range of instruments – you can even upload your own and teach other users!

D deepmusic.net

If you're just starting out playing music and need help, the short, easy-to-follow clips on deepmusic.net are exactly what you need. Or pick a show in your area to see your favourite musicians performing, then upload your own review of it afterwards. Every week there's a new set of fun questions for you – test your musical knowledge!

E musictolistento.com

Set up by the musical instrument shop of the same name, musictolistento.com has everything – from journalists' opinions on the latest songs and albums to lists of qualified music teachers and classes all over the country for all kinds of instruments. There are also articles on a range of international bands and musicians.

F musicmusic.net

musicmusic.net has a good section on music through history, though the information is mainly about music from before the fifteenth century. You can discuss anything related to music on the site with other fans. There's also a useful section on understanding and playing written music.

G musicability.com

This site is popular with musicians wanting to show their work to a wider audience. There are hundreds of videos posted by talented young bands from around the world, and even a monthly prize for the one that has been most popular. The comments added by users underneath each video are interesting, too!

H songsandtunes.net

The perfect site for buying all kinds of musical instruments that people no longer want! And if you're a musician and want to show other people your work, why not film yourself or your band and post it onto the website for free? You can also read your favourite performers' answers to questions you've always wanted to ask.

Part 3

Questions 11–15

For each question, choose the correct answer.

Robert Allen – tour guide

Seven years ago, I was studying Tourism at college, but needed to find a part-time job as my course was rather expensive. After considering several options, I trained to become a weekend tour guide in my home city – Chicago, USA. This involved taking visitors around the city, and I was surprised to discover how much I enjoyed giving those tours. I got to see the city that I'd been living in my whole life through the eyes of tourists, and it felt like a new experience every time!

After finishing my studies, I decided to go into tour guiding full-time. Although I thought it would be quite simple, in fact when I researched what I had to do, I found out that to get a licence as a full-time tour guide I needed to know a lot more than I'd learnt so far. All city guides have to be able to answer hundreds of questions about the city, covering everything from local architecture and history to the rules of public transport. After several challenging but interesting months, I gained my tour-guide qualification and registered as an independent tour guide.

Tour guiding isn't just about knowing historical facts or making sure you don't lose anyone from your group in the crowds. There are many other necessary skills. You should be able to be entertaining and tell interesting stories, and above all, you need to be able to react to changing situations, for example, if a place that you thought was open is actually closed when you arrive, or a route changes. Tourists don't want to hear what the problems are or that they're missing out on something, they just want to enjoy a well-organised tour.

I need to make sure visitors are happy with my tours, otherwise they could post a negative review online. Like most tour guides, I realise that these reviews are really important, as good reviews attract more customers. That's why making tours fun and stress-free is essential. For me, the enthusiasm and energy I put into my job means that my reviews are usually very good, and my tours are often recommended to other visitors coming to Chicago.

11 Why did Robert decide to start working as a weekend tour guide?

- **A** to have more fun in his life
- **B** to see his city in the same way tourists did
- **C** to help pay for his studies
- **D** to show visitors how wonderful his city is

12 What does Robert say about becoming a full-time tour guide?

- **A** He already had all the knowledge he required.
- **B** He was surprised to discover what was involved.
- **C** He was afraid some tourists' questions might be too difficult.
- **D** He found it quite easy to get a licence.

13 What does Robert feel is the most important part of his job?

- **A** checking that nobody gets lost during the tour
- **B** solving the tourists' problems
- **C** giving tourists all the details of any changes
- **D** dealing with unexpected events during a tour

14 What does Robert say about the reviews he receives?

- **A** They affect how many people choose his tours.
- **B** His customers always enjoy reading them.
- **C** They show his tours are the most popular in Chicago.
- **D** They help him plan better tours for future visitors.

15 What would be a good introduction to this text?

A Robert Allen tells us about what he did to achieve his childhood ambition.

B Robert Allen talks about what happened when he moved to Chicago.

C Robert Allen describes how his love of tour guiding developed into a career.

D Robert Allen explains why it's particularly hard to become a city tour guide in Chicago.

Part 4

Questions 16–20

Five sentences have been removed from the text below.
For each question, choose the correct answer.
There are three extra sentences which you do not need to use.

An underwater photo-journalist talks about his job

As an underwater photo-journalist, I've spent thousands of hours taking photographs beneath the ocean waves, and producing pictures and articles for magazines and TV. My work's taken me to many countries, where I've photographed and written about some of the most amazing ocean animals that exist. Being an underwater photo-journalist, however, isn't just about taking beautiful pictures. **16** _____

I spend a lot of time researching animals that live in the oceans. Before even starting to plan a new article, I consider which ones are important or interesting for people to read about; for example, species that are becoming increasingly rare, or less well-known creatures. **17** _____ Then I need to find out things like the best places to find that creature and the best time of year to go there.

Understanding animal behaviour is obviously important when it comes to underwater photography, so it's essential that I research that properly too. Apart from reading scientific journals, I speak to experts who spend their lives working with a particular species. **18** _____ Occasionally, I've even included these experts in the final published article.

My favourite animals to photograph and write about are whales and sharks. On one trip, I was photographing a species of whale which had rarely seen humans underwater before. **19** _____ But, to my surprise, I discovered that these whales were amazingly curious and trusting. Sharks are also wonderful to photograph – they're so powerful and move through the water so beautifully. **20** _____ I think that's a shame, and as a journalist, I have the opportunity to show what they're really like; if people understood them better, I'm sure they'd respect them, and not be so afraid of them.

A	It was an unknown situation for me and I didn't know what to expect.
B	However, studying them certainly helped me take great photographs on the trip.
C	It can actually take me up to a year to make a decision.
D	It's useful to go to these places with other photographers.
E	I sometimes invite them to come on a photographic trip to see what I do.
F	Despite this, people often have a negative view of these animals.
G	It also involves studying a wide variety of creatures.
H	They wanted to find out more about me.

Part 5

Questions 21–26

For each question, choose the correct answer.

The pink Amazon River dolphin

A special type of dolphin can be found in the waters of the Amazon River in Brazil. These dolphins are **(21)** .... from other species because they are pink. Scientists are not certain about the **(22)** .... for their skin colour, but some experts believe it could be a result of the red-coloured sand in the river. However, other scientists think that the dolphins **(23)** .... pinker as they become older.

Another special **(24)** .... about these dolphins is that they can **(25)** .... their heads from side to side, while most species of dolphin cannot. In addition, they have hairs on their noses that help them **(26)** .... for food at the bottom of the river. These animals are an amazing sight, and are popular with visitors and tourists travelling on the Amazon River by boat.

21	**A** unusual	**B** different	**C** opposite	**D** unknown
22	**A** aim	**B** idea	**C** answer	**D** reason
23	**A** increase	**B** develop	**C** improve	**D** grow
24	**A** fact	**B** information	**C** knowledge	**D** reality
25	**A** switch	**B** change	**C** turn	**D** fix
26	**A** catch	**B** find	**C** get	**D** search

Part 6

Questions 27–32

For each question, write the correct answer.
Write **one** word for each gap.

Spanish conversation club

We're a group of people aged 16–25 who meet every week for two hours of chat in Spanish. You don't have to be able to speak much Spanish: we welcome beginners, too. We talk about anything **(27)** .... may interest people, from food people enjoy **(28)** .... literature and politics.

We meet between 4.30 p.m. **(29)** .... 6.30 p.m. every Tuesday, in a large, comfortable room in the Central Library. The sessions are free, but we do ask people to pay £1 a session for coffee or juice. Staff from the School of Tourism at the University set **(30)** .... the group three years ago, but it's now organised **(31)** .... volunteers. The number of members **(32)** .... grown a lot during this time. As well as allowing people to practise their Spanish, the club brings people from different backgrounds together in order to enjoy each other's company.

WRITING (45 minutes)

Part 1

You **must** answer this question.
Write your answer in about **100 words** on the answer sheet.

Question 1

Read this email from your English-speaking college classmate Chris and the notes you have made.

EMAIL

From:	Chris
To:	All students
Subject:	Party for Mr Wright

Hi everyone

As you know, our teacher, Mr Wright, is leaving the college after teaching here for 15 years. Because Mr Wright's such a great teacher, I think we should organise a party for him. — *Good idea!*

We can either have the party inside the college or in the park. Which do you think would be better? — *Tell Chris*

Shall we all bring some food to the party? — *Yes, because ...*

It would be nice to give him a really special present. What can we give him? — *Suggest ...*

Chris

Write your **email** to Chris using **all the notes**.

Part 2

Choose **one** of these questions.
Write your answer in about **100 words** on the answer sheet.

Question 2

You see this announcement on an English-language website.

> **Articles wanted!**
>
> **Sport and exercise**
>
> What kind of exercise do you like doing?
> Do you think it's more enjoyable to watch sport or take part in it? Why?
>
> We'll put the most interesting articles answering these questions on our website!

Write your **article**.

Question 3

Your English teacher has asked you to write a story.
Your story must begin with this sentence.

Alex walked out of the airport into the hot sunshine.

Write your **story**.

LISTENING (approximately 30 minutes)

Part 1

Questions 1–7

For each question, choose the correct answer.

---

1 What has the woman left behind?

A

B

C

2 Which T-shirt does the boy want?

A

B

C

3 How did the woman book tickets for the show?

A

B

C

4 Why is the train to Histon delayed?

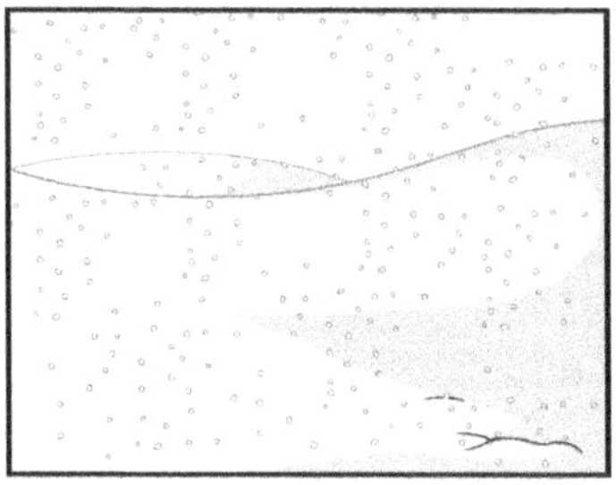

A

B

C

5 Where are the tourists most likely to see a tiger?

A

B

C

6 Which film will they go and see?

A

B

C

7 How did the man travel to work?

A

B

C

Part 2

Questions 8–13

For each question, choose the correct answer.

---

8 You will hear a husband and wife talking about keeping fit and healthy.
What do they both agree to change?

A their sleep routines

B their eating habits

C their exercise programmes

9 You will hear two friends talking about the woman's work.
How does the woman feel?

A She's pleased to have a new boss.

B She's excited about some recent changes.

C She's more positive than she was before.

10 You will hear a man telling a friend about his holiday.
How did the man feel when he visited some ancient ruins?

A surprised not to be able to climb them

B disappointed by their location

C impressed by their size

11 You will hear two friends talking about doing a foreign language course.
What do they agree about?

A which level of course to take

B where to take the course

C how long the course should be

12 You will hear two people talking about a music festival they're organising.
They're both worried about

A how good the music will be.

B how many people will attend.

C how suitable the weather will be.

13 You will hear two friends discussing an article about air pollution.
The woman is

A surprised by some new information.

B annoyed by the writer's attitude.

C confused by all the details.

Part 3

Questions 14–19

For each question, write the correct answer in the gap.
Write **one** or **two words** or a **number** or a **date** or a **time**.

You will hear a woman talking to some cyclists about a group bike ride.

Group bike ride

The group bike ride will be on **(14)** .... next week.

The length of the bike ride will be **(15)** ....

The bike ride will begin from **(16)** .... Bridge.

The cyclists will stop beside the **(17)** .... to rest and eat something.

Riders can buy **(18)** .... at a shop during the ride.

The cyclists must wear **(19)** ....

Part 4

Questions 20–25

For each question, choose the correct answer.

You will hear an interview with a wildlife photographer called James Thomson who has won a photography competition.

20 What made James become interested in photography?

A receiving a camera as a gift
B seeing his mother taking photographs
C attending a photography exhibition

21 What does James say about the park where he took his prize-winning photo?

A He had taken photos in it before.
B Someone he knew recommended it to him.
C It's always been well known for its natural beauty.

22 After winning the competition, James felt

A keen to tell his parents about his achievement.
B pleased to meet a famous photographer.
C surprised because he hadn't won in previous competitions.

23 In James' opinion, what is most important for a good photograph?

A It needs plenty of planning.
B It must be beautiful to look at.
C It teaches people something new.

24 James thinks that photography is a good hobby because

A it involves travelling to interesting places.
B it can become a successful career.
C it's a great social activity.

25 What advice does James have for other photographers?

A Spend a lot of time taking pictures.
B Do a course to get the right skills.
C Get the best equipment possible.

Test 2

READING (45 minutes)

Part 1

Questions 1–5

For each question, choose the correct answer.

1

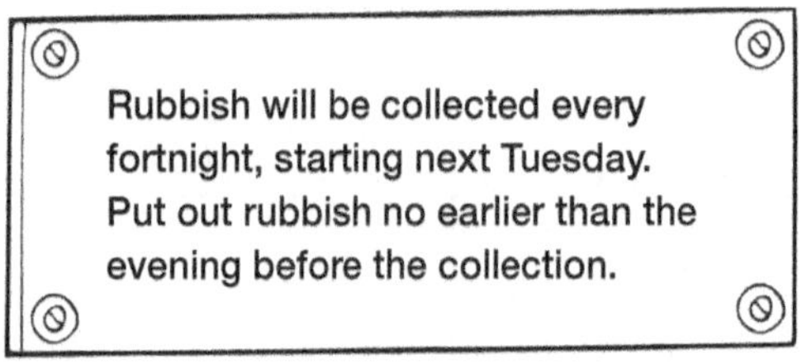

A Remember to put out your rubbish before Monday evening.

B Rubbish will be collected every Tuesday, starting next week.

C There will be a rubbish collection every two weeks.

2

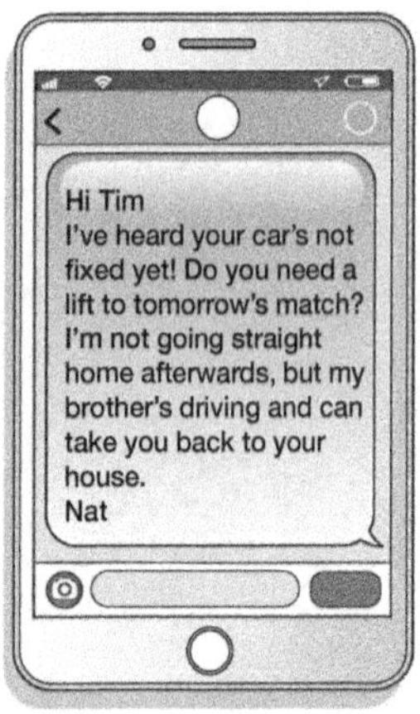

A Nat is explaining that his brother can give Tim a lift home after the match.

B Nat is asking whether Tim's car will be fixed before the match.

C Nat is reminding Tim that his brother is taking them to the match tomorrow.

3

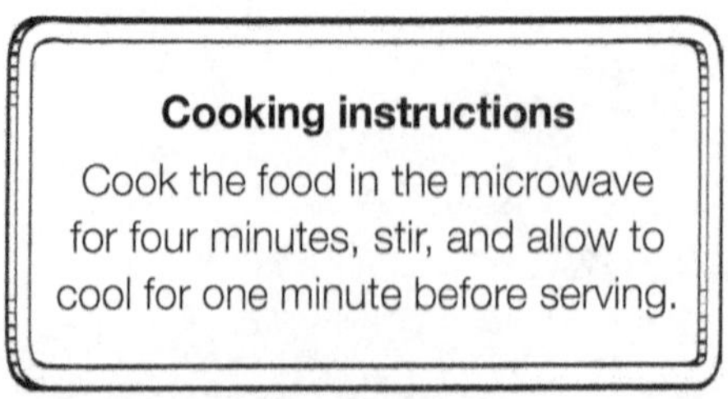

What does the label say?

A You should stir the food for one minute as it's cooling.

B You should leave the food for one minute after stirring it.

C You should cook the food then eat it after four minutes.

4

From : Mrs Walker
To : All fashion students'

So far, I've received some fantastic designs, but very few other ideas for our annual fashion show. Please contact me about how you'd like to run it. It's your show!

What does Mrs Walker want students to do?

A give their opinions on her ideas for the fashion show

B become more involved in organising the fashion show

C produce more designs for the fashion show

5

Claude

Sorry – there aren't any tickets left for tomorrow's play, but I left my number in case any are returned to the theatre. But there are plenty of seats left for the cinema!

Sandra

A Sandra is going to phone and get tickets for a trip to the cinema.

B Sandra is expecting both the play and the film to be very popular.

C Tickets might become available for something the friends hoped to see.

Part 2

Questions 6–10

For each question, choose the correct answer.

The people below all want to choose a place to have a party.
On the opposite page there are eight descriptions of places to have a party.
Decide which place would be the most suitable for the people below.

6 Jane is planning a very small party for her friends, and wants it to be in a historic place. She would like a photographer to be provided.

7 Colin and Alison want to hire a whole building just for themselves and their guests. They'd like the place to have a professional party organiser to help them plan everything, including an excellent meal.

8 Alex and Diana would like to arrive at their party by boat, and they want somewhere without bright lights. They're looking for a place which has had good reviews.

9 Peter needs a place where elderly guests can move around without difficulty, which also offers accommodation. He wants the choice of having the party either indoors or outdoors, depending on the weather on the day.

10 Jenny and Robin want a place where they can bring food themselves, and where children can run around and have fun. Some of their guests will need help with transport to the party.

Places to hold a party

A Hotel Homewood

Homewood is all on the ground floor, including guest bedrooms and all party facilities, to allow access for everyone. The beautiful hall will be available to you for your party, as well as the lovely gardens – watch boats go past on the river as you enjoy your celebration.

B Murphy's

Murphy's will provide a party expert to help you arrange your event. You won't need to share the venue with anyone, as the place will be all yours for the day. Our experienced staff will serve top-quality dishes and help keep young children entertained.

C Bruton Hall

At Bruton Hall, you can choose from a range of options, depending on your budget. For example, you can hire one of our chefs for the day or do the cooking yourselves. Our party guests get discounts on accommodation at several local hotels, all of which have had really good reviews.

D Waterford Hotel

Whether you want to let our chefs amaze you, or to provide your own refreshments, a party in this magnificent old building is an event to remember. Our staff can organise a taxi for anyone who requires one. We also have a fantastic playground for younger guests.

E Kite Lodge

It's possible to sail to the front door of Kite Lodge in the historic harbour. Kite Lodge was built in 1537 and the party room is lit only by candles, which is perfect for amazing photos of your event. Look online to see all the positive comments about previous events held here.

F The Priory Hotel

We have a team of staff to help with your celebration or event, including a prize-winning party planner, top chefs and our own photographer. We work hard to ensure that all guests, including kids and older visitors, have a fabulous time. There are 63 double bedrooms, all with easy access. So why not come and talk to us?

G Freshford Farm

Set in gorgeous countryside, it can be hard to believe that the airport is just a 10-minute drive away. Freshford Farm now has a specially built party hall, with glass walls allowing light in, so photos taken inside look as though they were taken outside! And children will love seeing the farm animals on site.

H Savernake House

The magnificent Savernake House dates back to the 18th century, and will look amazing in your party photos. We can even arrange for someone to take those for you, and capture the fantastic atmosphere! Unlike many places, we don't have a minimum number of guests.

Part 3

Questions 11–15

For each question, choose the correct answer.

Being a volunteer in Thailand

My name's Ella, and I'm 22. Last year I went to Thailand for two weeks with my sister Josie. Despite her being five years younger than me, our relationship isn't too bad. We went to help as part of a group of volunteers at an elephant sanctuary – a place where people look after sick and rescued elephants. To be honest, I wasn't sure at first if we would have much in common with the rest of the group because they were all much older than us. We were also nervous because it was the first time we'd done anything like that. In the end, though, there was no need to worry.

One of our main jobs at the sanctuary was to collect the elephants' food. Elephants eat huge amounts of grass and banana plants, so collecting this took most of the day. Josie found it really hard work, but to see the elephants enjoying their meal meant that, for me, it was worth it. We also helped wash the elephants in the river using big brushes and soap. I found that so much fun, even if I got wetter than the elephants did! The part of the day I most looked forward to was the evening. By the light of the moon, we led the elephants on foot into the forest area where they spent the night.

All the volunteers stayed in the same house. Josie and I shared a bedroom, so we didn't have much space. That was our decision, though, as Josie didn't want to be on her own. It was hot and humid, especially at night, but we'd expected that. The meals were delicious – and didn't include meat or fish, which neither of us is keen on. After dinner, all the volunteers and staff spent the evenings talking and playing games.

Now that we're back in the UK, Josie doesn't often talk about Thailand. But if anyone asks her if she enjoyed her time at the sanctuary, she says she loved it. However, I'm not sure she's being completely honest. I think she's probably a bit annoyed with herself now that she didn't take full advantage of her time there because she was missing her friends too much. But when she looks back, she can see how lucky she was to go there. Maybe she'll go back one day – I certainly will!

11 To begin with, Ella wondered whether she and Josie would

A get on well with the other volunteers.

B be scared of the elephants.

C argue with each other sometimes.

D find two weeks looking after elephants too long.

12 What was Ella's favourite activity?

A cleaning the elephants

B feeding the elephants

C walking with the elephants

D preparing food for the elephants

13 Ella says she was happy that

A the bedroom was big enough for them.

B the games they played were fun.

C the food they ate was vegetarian.

D the weather was generally good.

14 Ella thinks that Josie now

A enjoys telling people about their trip.

B realises that the trip was a great opportunity.

C misses everyone she met in Thailand.

D feels excited that she might go back to Thailand.

15 What would Ella write in a blog about her time in Thailand?

A We had a wonderful time – we relaxed, ate tasty meals and went for exciting elephant rides.

B We visited all the main tourist attractions and saw elephants and other wild animals in the beautiful forests.

C We visited a place where we could watch as elephants were fed. We were surprised how much food they needed.

D We had a great time taking care of some elephants. It was fantastic to be so close to them in the water.

Part 4

Questions 16–20

Five sentences have been removed from the text below.
For each question, choose the correct answer.
There are three extra sentences which you do not need to use.

The clever design of supermarkets

Most people don't realise how cleverly designed many big supermarkets around the world are. This careful planning includes where each of the products is located, the lights, the music, everything!

The first thing people in many countries may notice as they walk into large supermarkets is that getting into the store is much easier than getting out. **16** ______ This means that customers end up having to walk through half of the store to find a way out, seeing more things they want to buy on the way.

Once they're inside, the first products many shoppers often see are fruit and vegetables. **17** ______ If that were the case, fruit and vegetables, many of which are easily damaged, could be put on top of the other shopping. But having them near the entrance can make customers feel that everything in the store is fresh and healthy, encouraging them to buy more.

What customers might also notice as they enter is the smell of freshly baked bread. This attracts many people towards the bakery to buy some. **18** ______ Putting it in this location makes sure that shoppers walk past as many other products as possible to reach their delicious bread.

Research shows that if music is played in supermarkets, customers slow down and spend more time shopping. **19** ______ And supermarkets know, of course, that this also means they'll buy more products.

In some countries, when customers finally arrive at the queue for the checkouts, they find themselves face-to-face with shelves full of small, inexpensive products like chocolate and sweets. **20** ______ So they're often bought by tired parents to keep their bored sons or daughters entertained as they pack their shopping. Products placed next to checkouts sell up to eight times faster than in other parts of a store.

A	In one study, they actually stayed 34% longer than if there was none.
B	As a result, shoppers pass the cheaper products more quickly.
C	That's why expensive products are placed at the same height as people's eyes.
D	In fact, it would be more convenient for customers to reach this section later.
E	Many of these are designed to attract children.
F	That's because they often have entry doors that can't be used as exits.
G	This would encourage customers and their children to leave the store too quickly.
H	However, it's often right at the back of the store.

Part 5

Questions 21–26

For each question, choose the correct answer.

Future foods

The world is always looking for new methods of food production. Scientists in Australia are now **(21)** .... in a project to grow food in a different way.

The scientists have produced plants that have grown not just faster, but also bigger. They **(22)** .... their techniques on methods that were previously tried in experiments to grow crops in space. Crops like peas were grown in special glass houses where temperatures were carefully controlled. Special lights were shone on the young plants for 22 hours a day. This had the **(23)** .... of increasing the speed at which the plants developed.

The scientists say that the results were even better than they had hoped. When they **(24)** .... the plants with ones grown in **(25)** .... conditions, they found that the new plants were also much healthier. Many people **(26)** .... that the technique will be used with a wide variety of plants in the future.

21	**A**	involved	**B**	concerned	**C**	decided	**D**	accepted
22	**A**	found	**B**	agreed	**C**	set	**D**	based
23	**A**	conclusion	**B**	solution	**C**	effect	**D**	product
24	**A**	recognised	**B**	looked	**C**	considered	**D**	compared
25	**A**	likely	**B**	general	**C**	normal	**D**	common
26	**A**	predict	**B**	tell	**C**	follow	**D**	communicate

Part 6

Questions 27–32

For each question, write the correct answer.
Write **one** word for each gap.

A rainy day

One summer's day, my family decided to visit a waterfall in the countryside near our town. As we walked across the fields towards the waterfall, we **(27)** .... see it in the distance. It was quite **(28)** .... long way, but we got there after about an hour. We sat down near the pool at the bottom of the waterfall to enjoy the picnic that we **(29)** .... taken with us. Then we noticed some black clouds in the sky, and some large drops **(30)** .... rain fell on us, so we quickly started to collect our things together. Soon the rain began **(31)** .... fall heavily. Carrying our bags, we ran as fast as we could, and when we reached the town, we went into the first café we saw. In **(32)** .... of our wet clothes, we soon felt better after a delicious drink of hot chocolate!

WRITING (45 minutes)

Part 1

You **must** answer this question.
Write your answer in about **100 words** on the answer sheet.

Question 1

Read this email from your English-speaking friend Mo and the notes you have made.

EMAIL

From: Mo

Subject: Day out

Hi,

We've been very busy recently, so I thought it would be nice to have a day out this weekend.

Agree

We could go to the beach or spend a day shopping in the city. Which would you prefer?

Say which

I think it would be nice to invite some other friends to come with us. What do you think?

Tell Mo

Afterwards, you could come to my house for dinner, if you're free. Let me know!

Thanks, but …

Mo

Write your **email** to Mo using **all the notes**.

Part 2

Choose **one** of these questions.
Write your answer in about **100 words** on the answer sheet.

Question 2

You see this announcement on an English-language website.

Articles wanted!

Learning English

If you are learning English, we want to hear from you.

What do you like about learning English?

What advice do you have for people who are starting to learn English?

We'll publish the most interesting articles answering these questions on our website.

Write your **article**.

Question 3

Your English teacher has asked you to write a story.
Your story must begin with this sentence.

Charlie felt happy as he opened the train door.

Write your **story**.

LISTENING (approximately 30 minutes)

Part 1

Questions 1–7

For each question, choose the correct answer.

---

1 What does the man decide to buy?

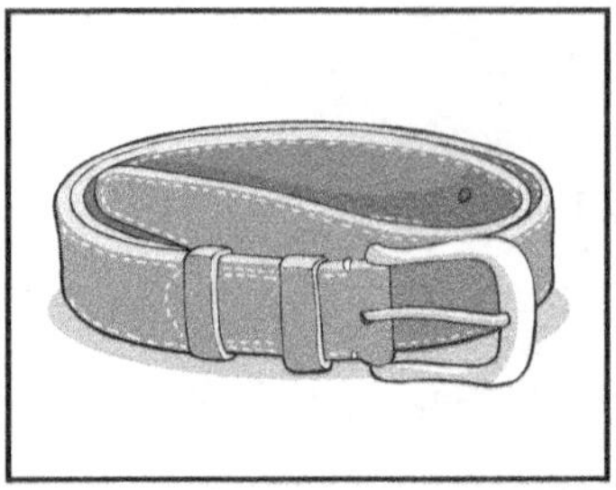

A

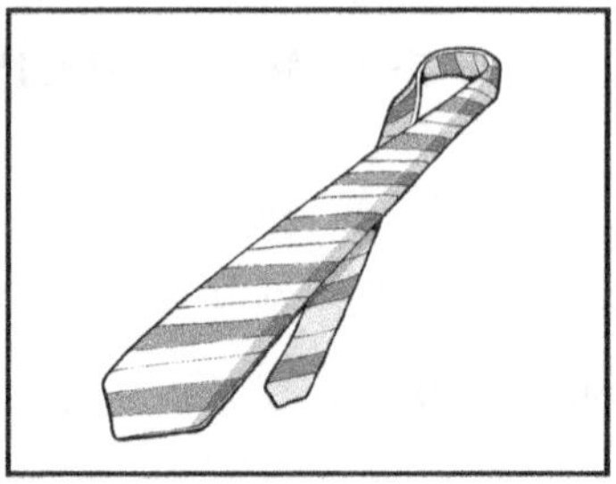

B

C

2 What kind of job has the woman applied for?

A

B

C

3 How will the man travel to work today?

A

B

C

4 Where does the man think he lost his wallet?

A

B

C

5 What will the man make for dinner tonight?

A

B

C

6 Who was the woman's favourite character in the film?

A

B

C

7 What does the girl want her father to deliver?

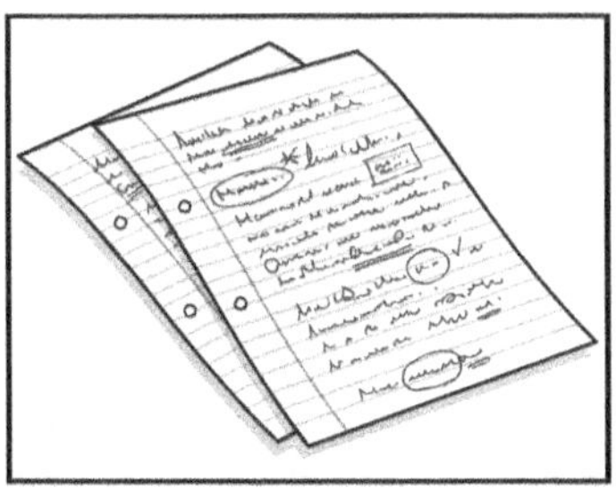

A

B

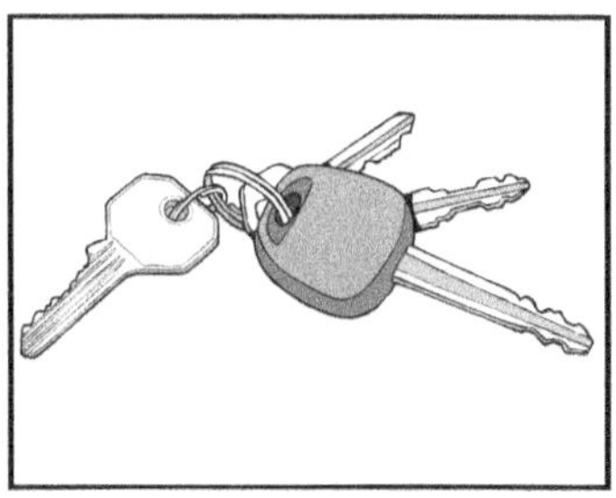

C

Part 2

Questions 8–13

For each question, choose the correct answer.

---

8 You will hear two friends talking about some work the man has to do.
The woman tells the man not to worry about

A how quickly he does the work.

B the order in which he does the work.

C having to ask for support from others.

9 You will hear two students talking about a history website.
They agree that

A it looks good.

B it's easy to use.

C it's useful for studying.

10 You will hear two friends talking about the woman's holiday.
How did she feel about it?

A satisfied with the food that she tried

B impressed with the hotel she stayed in

C pleased with the prices she paid for things

11 You will hear two friends talking about a shopping centre.
They agree that it needs to have

A extra space for parking.

B more places to eat.

C a wider range of shops.

12 You will hear two friends talking about playing golf.
What does the woman say about it?

A She hopes she'll be able to play it more often.

B She thinks the rules are too complicated.

C She believes she has a talent for it.

13 You will hear two friends talking about a novel.
What does the man say about it?

A The characters aren't very interesting.

B The chapters are too long.

C The story isn't very realistic.

Part 3

Questions 14–19

For each question, write the correct answer in the gap.
Write **one** or **two words** or a **number** or a **date** or a **time**.

You will hear some information about a one-day drumming class.

Japanese *Taiko* drumming class

Students will need to have a lot of **(14)** .... for the class.

Students will start the class by seeing a **(15)** .... before listening to a talk.

In the morning, students will learn to **(16)** .... correctly.

The afternoon session will focus on what are known as **(17)** ....

Drumming improves people's **(18)** .... and fitness.

The instructor's email address is **(19)** ....@taiko.uk.

Part 4

Questions 20–25

For each question, choose the correct answer.

You will hear an interview with a young woman called Lara Andrews, who has a baking business.

20 Why did Lara decide to open her baking business?

- **A** Her parents encouraged her to do it.
- **B** Her teacher thought she'd be successful.
- **C** Her school friends bought cakes from her.

21 What challenge did Lara have to deal with when she started her business?

- **A** managing her time
- **B** dealing with complaints
- **C** finding the right recipes

22 Lara says that baking bread is

- **A** more popular than making cakes.
- **B** more difficult than making cakes.
- **C** more fun than making cakes.

23 What does Lara feel that she needs to do to improve her business?

- **A** spend more money on advertising
- **B** sell more traditional products
- **C** develop more confidence in herself

24 What does Lara intend to do in the future?

- **A** have her own café
- **B** teach young people
- **C** write a book

25 Lara advises people who want to start a baking business to

- **A** learn from famous bakers.
- **B** get a qualification before they start.
- **C** be realistic about what they can achieve.

Test 3

READING (45 minutes)

Part 1

Questions 1–5

For each question, choose the correct answer.

1

Walking group
Start from Mill Café, Tuesday 10 a.m. Café has limited parking, but there's a public car park nearby. Remember a picnic lunch, or get one from the café if ordered a day in advance.

A The walkers are planning to have their lunch in Mill Café next Tuesday.

B If walkers want lunch from Mill Café, they must arrange this before Tuesday.

C Walking group members can't park in Mill Café car park on Tuesday.

2

Washing instructions
Think about the climate!
Save energy and wash at 30°C.
100% cotton. Wash with clothes of similar colours.

A Cotton clothes must be washed at 30°C.

B Wash different colours at different temperatures.

C Wash at this temperature to help the environment.

3

From : Dominico
To : Ana

I'm going to be delayed tonight because of traffic. Can you get the tickets as soon as you get to the cinema? Then we won't have to stand in a long queue.

What does the email say?

A Ana will miss the start of the film due to heavy traffic.

B Ana should try to buy the cinema tickets before Domenico arrives.

C Domenico and Ana can meet in the queue at the cinema.

4

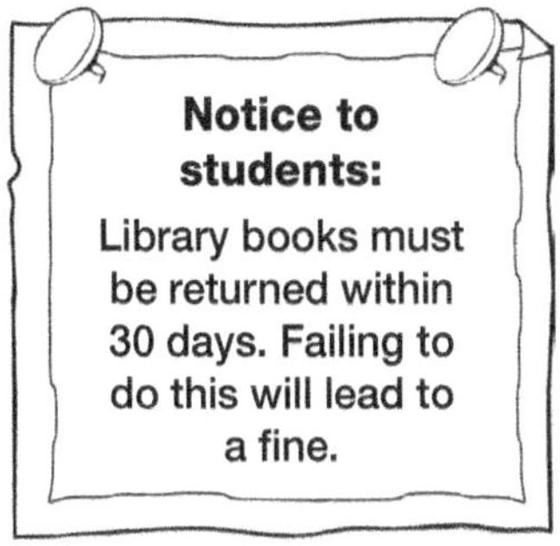

What does the notice say?

A Students will have to pay if they don't bring books back on time.

B Students can pay a small charge to borrow books for longer than 30 days.

C Students must not take out more books until they pay what they owe.

5

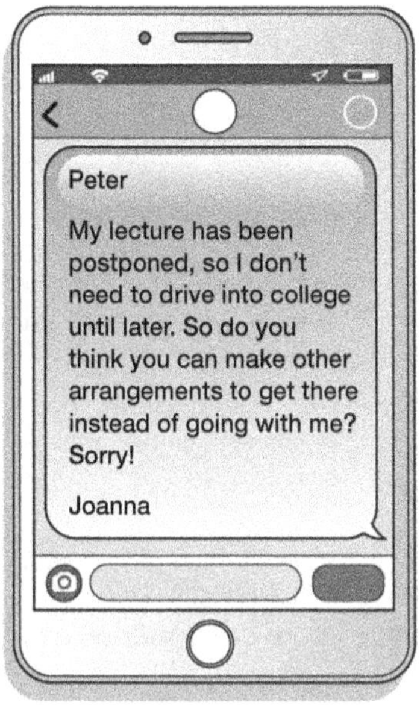

What is Joanna telling Peter?

A His college lecture is cancelled.

B She is able to offer him a lift to their college.

C He needs to find a different way to go to college.

Part 2

Questions 6–10

For each question, choose the correct answer.

The people below all want to go on an activity holiday.
On the opposite page there are eight advertisements for activity holidays.
Decide which activity holiday would be the most suitable for the people below.

6 

Asma loves cycling, but she also wants to be able to relax after a busy day. She'd like to try the local food while she's on holiday.

7 

Dan is a biology student and has an interest in sea life. He wants to try doing a few water sports. He'd like to sleep in a tent among trees.

8 

Tilda enjoys meeting new people, and likes hiking in the countryside. She wants to sleep somewhere comfortable, and doesn't like camping.

9 

Archie is looking for an activity-filled holiday where he can dive and swim. He's happy to stay in basic accommodation and cook his own meals. He's keen to try a fun or unusual local activity.

10 

Mia is very interested in nature, and would like to visit a place with wildlife that most people have never seen. She likes taking photos, and wants something sociable to do in the evenings.

Activity holidays

A Setty National Park

If you enjoy standing on a hill you've just walked up, far from any towns, looking at the views, then join us on the trip of a lifetime. You'll be with a group of walkers of similar ability to yours, and you'll have plenty of time to make friends. You'll spend every night in one of the area's top hotels.

B Adventure Trips

Our luxury accommodation is situated near the sea, with fantastic views of the mountains to the north. Activities include watching dolphins – the perfect photo opportunity – as well as sailing and surfing. Enjoy local culture evenings, where you'll find out more about what this region has to offer.

C Mari Resort

Mari Resort is located in pine forests on the coast. Here, you can have a go at sailing and surfing, and take a trip in a glass-bottomed boat to see the creatures beneath the waves. Stay in our peaceful campsite for a good night's sleep.

D North Island

Go back to nature and join us on our extreme hiking tour. At the end of each day, we'll cook together on the campfire with local ingredients and then enjoy the rest of the evening in peaceful surroundings, listening to the sounds of the waves.

E Sunshine Holidays

However you enjoy spending time in the water, you can do it with us. And in the evenings, why not learn a new skill? Performers from nearby villages come along to teach guests their unique style of dancing – we're sure you haven't done anything like this before! Stay in a simple wooden hut with a kitchen.

F Coral River

Come along on our cycling tour along the Coral River. Take photos of colourful parrots and flowers, and look forward to relaxing in style at the best hotels on our route. If you prefer, you can use local campsites instead.

G Terra Holidays

If you're more into biking than hiking, then this is the holiday for you! Enjoy the fresh air as we follow interesting routes through the mountains. Each lunchtime, we'll stop at a restaurant and taste typical dishes from the region. Then, after a long day, sit by the pool and enjoy a cool drink!

H Jungle Camp

Far away from everyday life, the Jungle Camp is the gateway to a whole new world. See plants and animals like nowhere else on Earth – don't forget your camera! Join everyone after dinner for board games, and spend the nights in a cosy tent.

Part 3

Questions 11–15

For each question, choose the correct answer.

Selling flowers

I'm Gina D'Costa and I run a flower shop in the UK. We don't just sell flowers to people buying them for friends or for their homes; all kinds of customers want flowers. Hotels and offices often have flowers in Reception, and sometimes we take part in photo sessions for businesses by providing flowers for their advertising pictures. Once I even decorated a castle with flowers for a wedding. It took a huge amount of work, but I was really proud of the job we'd done.

My day starts at 4 a.m. when I go to the market to buy fresh flowers. Most people are still asleep then and my friends think I must be crazy, but it's never bothered me – I'm excited about what I do. It's often colder than I'd like, and it's usually dark, but you can't expect anything else at that time in the morning, so I don't let it worry me.

The flower market's wonderful, with flowers from all over the world. The sights and smells make it hard to make a decision. If I was choosing for myself, I'd probably only get pink ones – it's my favourite colour. But I mustn't forget that what I love and what other people want aren't necessarily the same thing. It isn't always possible to find customers' choices – not all flowers are available all year. I'm not so keen on having to argue about prices with the flower-sellers, but it's a necessary part of the job. Flowers aren't cheap, so I have to try to get the best price possible.

Back at the shop we look at customer orders and set up vases with the flowers I've bought. Then we get on with creating bunches of flowers and working out how much orders will cost. Customers are often surprised by how expensive they are, and I sometimes have to ask them to think again about what they'd like. Some people might think this sounds like too much trouble, but I like thinking about how I can put together the nicest possible flowers for the amount of money someone wants to spend. That's what you have to do when you're selling things – I wouldn't want any other job!

11 In the first paragraph, what does Gina say about her work?

- **A** She was especially pleased with one project she was involved in.
- **B** She finds visiting other businesses very interesting.
- **C** She has learnt how to take good photographs of her flowers.
- **D** She prefers some types of customers to others.

12 What does Gina say about getting up so early?

- **A** She admits she needs more sleep.
- **B** She doesn't notice what the weather's like.
- **C** Her friends don't realise how hard it is for her.
- **D** It's worth doing because she loves her job.

13 What does Gina find difficult when she is at the flower market?

- **A** asking to pay less for flowers
- **B** finding flowers in a variety of colours
- **C** remembering what customers have asked for
- **D** having such a limited range of flowers to choose from

14 When working in her shop, Gina feels

- **A** guilty about the high prices she has to charge.
- **B** upset when people change their mind.
- **C** pleased she is able to sell so many flowers.
- **D** positive about the challenges she has to deal with.

15 Which would be a good notice for the window of Gina's flower shop?

A All our flowers are locally grown!

B We can provide flowers for any occasion – large or small!

C Design your own flower display here!

D We can find any kind of flower that you'd like!

Part 4

Questions 16–20

Five sentences have been removed from the text below.
For each question, choose the correct answer.
There are three extra sentences which you do not need to use.

A very original artist

Jenny Blatchford, the talented young sculptor, was born in the south-west of England in 1989. She is the daughter of a doctor, and the family lived in a number of different towns when Jenny was a child. **16** ______ However, there were some advantages; she says it gave her the ability to become used to new environments very quickly.

Her earliest memories are of playing with her primary school friends on the outskirts of a city where workers were building lots of new apartment blocks. **17** ______ The amount of skill involved impressed her greatly, and Jenny says that this early experience led her to become interested in sculpture.

She was a clever student and went to a very good school. It was a wonderful place to study science and languages, but not art. **18** ______ In fact, most of the staff thought it was something pupils were either good or bad at, and didn't need special instruction. Luckily one of her teachers recognised Jenny's talent and gave her art lessons in the evenings after school.

No-one was surprised when Jenny chose to apply to study art at college. She had the opportunity to develop her skills in sculpture, creating huge statues of animals, mainly out of materials such as wood, stone and metal. **19** ______ Recently she has even started to make them out of paper. Some of her sculptures are extremely realistic, but others are unusually shaped. Art experts love her originality and she has won many awards and prizes.

Jenny gets her ideas for her sculptures in a number of different ways. **20** ______ She also likes to look at other people's art. She says the most important thing is that she is excited by each new project.

A	Sometimes they come from spending time outdoors.
B	This meant that she didn't have the chance to get to know anywhere very well.
C	In spite of this, she is influencing a lot of young artists.
D	Unfortunately, little time was spent there on teaching it.
E	She loved moving around, and made many new friends.
F	However, she also enjoyed trying to use other things, like glass.
G	All subjects were taught very well, and Jenny learned quickly.
H	She loved watching as each new floor was added.

Part 5

Questions 21–26

For each question, choose the correct answer.

Plastic in the oceans

These days, plastic waste in the world's oceans has become a serious issue. Scientists want people to know about the problems that are created by the plastic that gets into the oceans, often after people have used it and **(21)** .... it away. Many of these bits of plastic are extremely small; some are just the **(22)** .... of a tiny piece of salt.

These little pieces of plastic often **(23)** .... up in the sea. There, perhaps because they look very similar to fish eggs, they are often eaten by other animals. They are also sometimes **(24)** .... by sea creatures who are trying to feed their own young. Scientists say that this is very bad for many different **(25)** .... of animal; cod, penguins and dolphins have all been **(26)** .... by the problem.

21	**A** taken	**B** given	**C** thrown	**D** put
22	**A** amount	**B** size	**C** total	**D** quantity
23	**A** keep	**B** grow	**C** end	**D** catch
24	**A** looked	**B** hunted	**C** searched	**D** collected
25	**A** members	**B** ranges	**C** species	**D** names
26	**A** approached	**B** affected	**C** arranged	**D** attended

Part 6

Questions 27–32

For each question, write the correct answer.
Write **one** word for each gap.

The Westway Cinema

The new Westway Cinema is finally open! I went last night with my brother, and we both agreed it's much better than the old one **(27)** .... to be. Although the ticket prices are higher, the extra cost is worth paying.

The new owners **(28)** .... now taken out all the old seats and put in brand new ones that are really comfortable. There's also new air conditioning. This is fantastic because in the past it was sometimes **(29)** .... hot that it was difficult to concentrate on the film!

There are also special offers available. For example, **(30)** .... you buy two tickets, you can choose something for free – either a snack or a drink. I'm sure this **(31)** .... be popular, as you can't bring **(32)** .... own food into the cinema.

I'd really recommend going to the Westway Cinema – it's a great night out.

WRITING (45 minutes)

Part 1

You **must** answer this question.
Write your answer in about **100 words** on the answer sheet.

Question 1

Read this email from your English-speaking friend Eden and the notes you have made.

EMAIL

From: Eden

Subject: Cycling on Tuesday evening

Hi,

I'm really looking forward to going cycling with you on Tuesday evening. I hope you still want to go! — *Of course!*

There are two cycle routes near where I live. We could cycle through the forest or we could cycle round the lake. Which would you prefer? — *Explain*

Do you think we should take some food with us? — *Tell Eden*

Do you have time to come to my house and watch a film afterwards? — *No, because …*

Reply soon!

Eden

Write your **email** to Eden using **all the notes**.

Part 2

Choose **one** of these questions.
Write your answer in about **100 words** on the answer sheet.

Question 2

You see this announcement on an English-language website.

> **Articles wanted!**
>
> # Friends
>
> How important is it to be in contact with friends every day? Is it important to meet your friends face to face or can you stay friends by just chatting online?
>
> The best articles answering these questions will win a prize.

Write your **article**.

Question 3

Your English teacher has asked you to write a story.
Your story must begin with this sentence.

By the time I arrived, there were already lots of people at the party.

Write your **story**.

LISTENING (approximately 30 minutes)

Part 1

Questions 1–7

For each question, choose the correct answer.

---

1 What did the man do yesterday?

A

B

C

2 How did the woman travel back from her holiday?

A

B

C

3 Which hat did the fashion model wear in the photos?

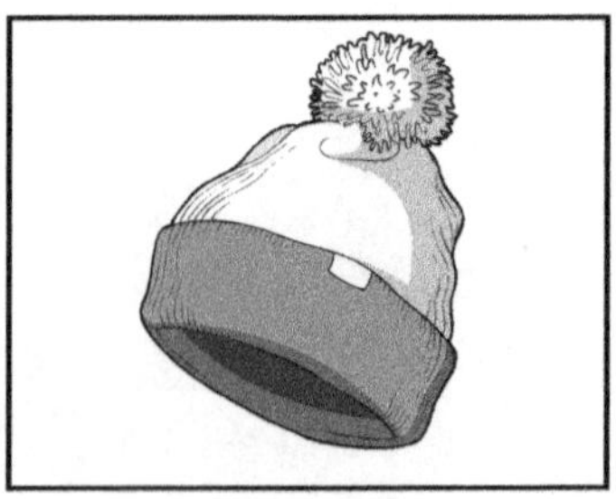

A

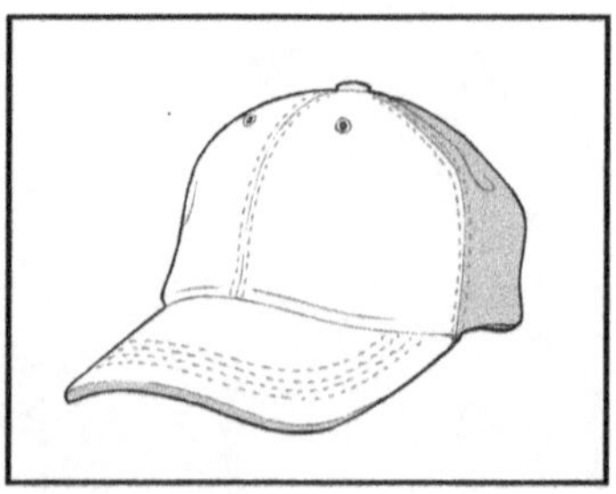

B

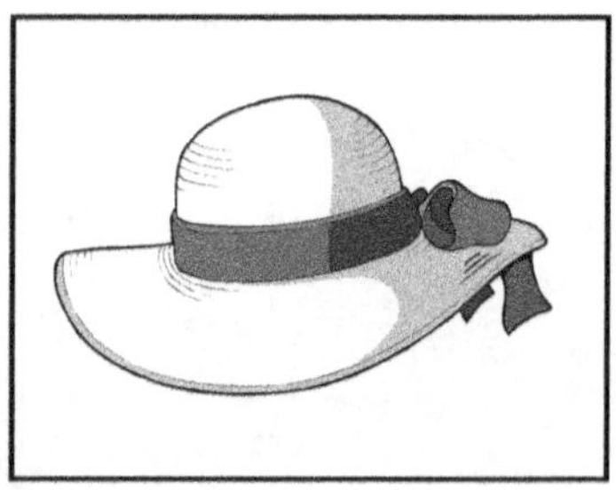

C

4 Where did the man leave his driving licence?

A

B

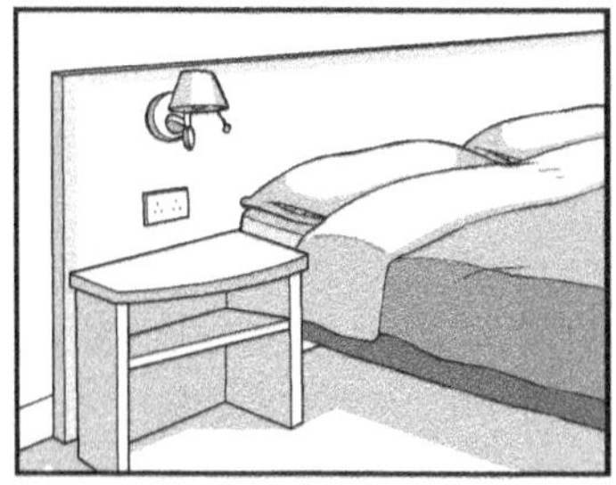

C

5 Where are they going walking?

A

B

C

6 What will the woman do to her friend's car?

A

B

C

7 What did the woman eat at the restaurant?

A

B

C

Part 2

Questions 8–13

For each question, choose the correct answer.

---

8 You will hear two friends talking about the woman's dress.
Why is the woman returning the dress to the shop?

A It's the wrong colour.

B It's damaged.

C It doesn't fit.

9 You will hear two friends talking about a new sports centre.
They agree that it needs to have

A more staff available.

B better equipment.

C bigger changing rooms.

10 You will hear a woman talking to a receptionist in a hotel.
Why has the woman gone to the hotel?

A to book a room

B to meet someone

C to make a complaint

11 You will hear a man telling a friend about his holiday in the mountains.
What did he enjoy most about it?

A having skiing lessons

B seeing the countryside

C spending time with friends

12 You will hear two friends talking about playing the guitar.
What's the man going to do?

A practise playing with other people

B start playing a different instrument

C try to play every day

13 You will hear two friends talking about a film they've just seen.
What does the man say about the film?

A It wasn't very funny.

B It won an important prize.

C It was easy to predict the ending.

Part 3

Questions 14–19

For each question, write the correct answer in the gap.
Write **one** or **two words** or a **number** or a **date** or a **time**.

You will hear an announcement about a song writing competition.

Song writing competition

Songs in this year's competition must be about the **(14)** ....

Songs must be no longer than **(15)** ....

The judge this year is a famous **(16)** ....

The prize for the winner is a trip to a **(17)** ....

The closing date for entries is **(18)** ....

The email address to send songs to is **(19)** ....@songwriters.net

Part 4

Questions 20–25

For each question, choose the correct answer.

You will hear an interview with a professional explorer called Alexis Bartoli, who travels to places that few other people visit.

20 Alexis decided to become an explorer after

A reading a book.

B listening to a talk.

C seeing a TV programme.

21 Alexis felt anxious before his first expedition because

A he didn't know what to expect.

B he knew it would be quite dangerous.

C he'd never been very far away from home.

22 Why did Alexis start making films on his expeditions?

A to make money for future trips

B to provide scientists with information

C to learn a new skill

23 Alexis says his favourite part of any expedition is

A discovering new landscapes.

B experiencing different climates.

C meeting new people.

24 Alexis's latest expedition involved

A walking across a desert.

B sailing across an ocean.

C spending time in a rainforest.

25 What does Alexis say he wants to do in the future?

A try a different profession

B explore his home country

C return to places he's visited before

Test 4

READING (45 minutes)

Part 1

Questions 1–5

For each question, choose the correct answer.

1

Why did Joanne write this email?

A to pass on an invitation

B to make a suggestion

C to change an arrangement

2

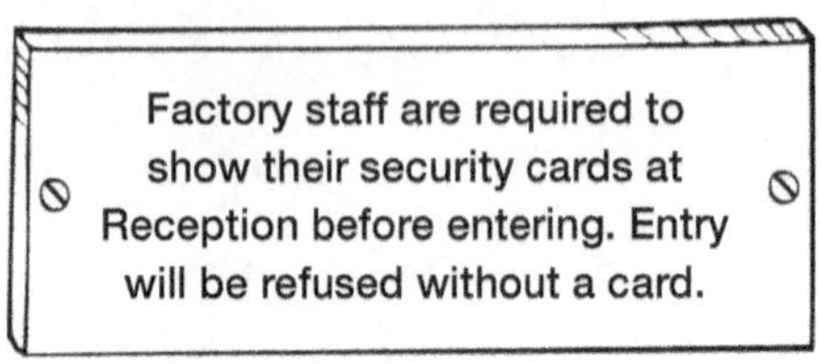

What does the notice say?

A Staff cannot enter unless they have a card.

B Staff requiring a card can apply at Reception.

C Staff with a card may still be refused entry.

3

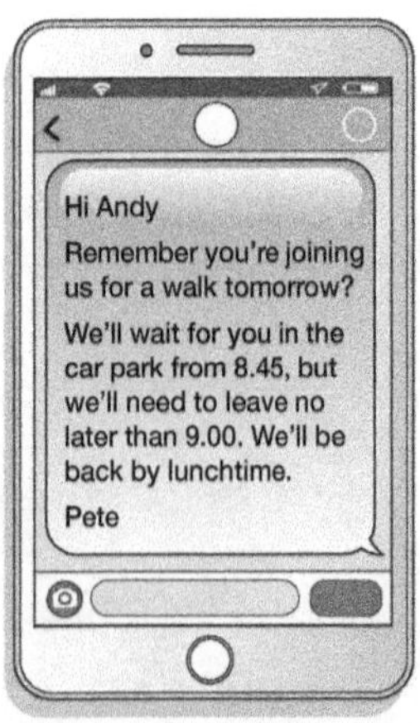

What is Pete doing?

A informing Andy that there's a walk tomorrow

B warning Andy not to be late for the walk

C enquiring whether Andy can come on the walk

4

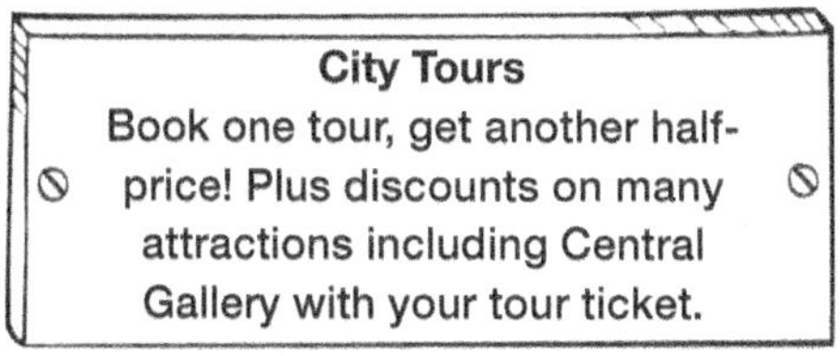

A The Central Gallery offers tours at a good price to all visitors.

B Two people can go on a city tour for the price of one.

C People on the tour can buy cheaper tickets for various places in the city.

5

Ben is

A grateful for Margo's suggestion.

B excited about trying a new activity.

C looking forward to seeing Margo.

Part 2

Questions 6–10

For each question, choose the correct answer.

The people below all want to improve their cooking skills.
On the opposite page there are eight advertisements for cooking classes.
Decide which class would be the most suitable for the people below.

6 

Rashid would like to cook healthy meals for his children, and is looking for a course which teaches basic skills. He and his children enjoy eating dishes from around the world.

7 

Angela's a good cook, and wants to make a special dinner for 20 guests at her husband's birthday party. She'd like to make more advanced dishes, and her husband particularly likes traditional food.

8 

Marcus would like some ideas for meals for one person, without having to buy fresh ingredients every day. He wants quick and easy dishes he can cook when he gets home from work feeling hungry.

9 

Francesca is an experienced cook who wants to get new ideas for meals for her family. She'd like to increase her range of skills in the kitchen and learn how to make tasty desserts.

10 

Aston wants to spend time trying complicated recipes at the weekend because he finds it relaxing. He wants to make food in large amounts, so he can take a proper meal to work for lunch every day.

Cooking classes

A Food for you

If you often eat away from home and want some food you can take with you, you'll be interested in our recipes for snacks that are quick and easy to make. We'll show you how to create delicious healthy treats and sweets – great for young and old alike on family picnics.

B Tasty treats

If you're just starting your journey to become a great cook, this course is for you! We'll teach you how to prepare food safely, and show you recipes for simple but tasty dishes from many different countries. People of all ages will enjoy these dishes, which are also very good for you.

C Come and cook!

Whether you're cooking for yourself or for others, our simple but delicious meals don't take long to make – perfect for those with busy lives. We'll show you how to make the most of what you've probably already got in your kitchen cupboards. Satisfying meals without too much trouble!

D Kerry's kitchen

This course is for less experienced cooks who want to create exciting meals. Perfect for special occasions or when you just fancy doing something different. Learn to create a meal from starter to dessert, and how to present it attractively for your dinner party guests. Our focus is on modern international dishes.

E Delicious dishes

This course is for people who want to take their cookery skills to the next level. We focus on typical recipes – especially for main courses – passed down through generations from all over the country, to help you put together a fantastic meal for any occasion. We promise everyone will be impressed!

F Eat well

Our main dishes and healthy desserts are challenging to prepare and cook, but they're definitely worth the effort. Once they're done, there's enough for you to divide up into several one-meal portions. Then you can keep them for a few days in the fridge until you need them.

G Food lovers

If you lead a busy life and don't particularly like making meals, come and find out how to feed family and friends simple food made from healthy, fresh ingredients. Our 'picnic suppers' involve baking delicious breads and cakes which you can prepare in advance, then serve with salads and other cold dishes.

H Hot stuff

You may consider yourself a bit of a chef, but there's always more to learn! Come on our course and we'll not only teach you advanced techniques but give you loads of interesting and unusual recipes – from soups to cakes and ice-cream – that even very young children will love.

Part 3

Questions 11–15

For each question, choose the correct answer.

My film club

By Sebastian Walters

My city has a typical modern cinema showing all the latest films I want to see, and lots of films for kids at the weekends. It's around the corner from where I live, but a year ago, I realised something was missing – the experience of discussing a film in detail with a group of people after watching it with them. So, I persuaded two friends to join me and started a film club!

We decided early on that we didn't want to hire a cinema to show the films in. Instead, we choose a different location in the city each month. For example, we hired an old factory to show a film that was set in Antarctica. It was freezing cold, and this created the perfect atmosphere for the film, which was brilliant! Some places we use are even free, as the owners make money by selling snacks during the film, which means we can keep our prices low. We're happy to make enough to cover our costs – we're not trying to make a profit.

Each time we show a film, everything is a bit easier for us, especially now we've got our own reliable equipment. We also know the number of tickets we've sold because everything's online – no more concerns about empty seats! There's still always plenty to do, but when people of all ages come up at the end to say what a great experience they've had, it's wonderful.

The website's been a great help, and we're now in contact with other film clubs all over the country. We've been to see how people do things in different places – but it's always good to get back to our own club again! We've started a blog, too, because we know that most people now go online for information about films, rather than read reviews in local papers. We've also tried putting up a few posters in cafés. Nothing's as successful as word of mouth, though – people recommending us to their friends. And the audience love the surprise activities we put on with each film – last month it was a movie quiz, which everybody enjoyed.

11 Why did Sebastian decide to start a film club?

A He didn't like the films at his local cinema.

B He wanted the opportunity to share opinions about films.

C The nearest cinema was too far from his house.

D His friends suggested the idea to him.

12 Why does Sebastian show films in many different places?

A He wants to make as much money as possible.

B He can offer a wider variety of food to audiences.

C He wants more people to be able to watch the films.

D He can choose somewhere suitable for each film.

13 How does Sebastian feel at each film club session now?

A anxious about how many people will come

B worried about some of the equipment not working properly

C pleased when he hears that the audience have enjoyed themselves

D happy to be able to relax completely

14 How do most people find out about the film club?

A They are told about it by someone they know.

B They notice posters in the local area.

C They see its social media page.

D They read about it in the local newspaper.

15 What would Sebastian write on the film club blog?

A You'll never guess what we're planning to do before the next film – it'll be something to get everyone talking for sure! Details to follow …

B We're planning to set up clubs all over the country because we've been so successful – watch this space!

C Our aim's to encourage a wider range of viewers. We get lots of children, but it's so important to include all ages.

D We've put up our ticket prices, but food and drinks are included in the price, so we think it's good value.

Part 4

Questions 16–20

Five sentences have been removed from the text below.
For each question, choose the correct answer.
There are three extra sentences which you do not need to use.

How the world's oldest message in a bottle found its way home

Staff at the Marine Biological Association (MBA) in England were surprised when an envelope arrived at their offices addressed to 'George Parker Bidder'. They couldn't understand why someone was writing to the Association's former president, who had been dead for more than 60 years. It became clearer when the envelope was opened and its contents examined. Inside, there was an old postcard. Written on one side was a series of questions about how the postcard had been discovered. **16** ______

It turned out that the postcard had come from a bottle dropped into the North Sea more than a century earlier. It was one of just over 1,000 bottles that Bidder had thrown into the water as part of a study into ocean currents and the movement of fish. **17** ______ They were generally picked up by fishermen or by people walking along the beach, who then sent the postcards inside them back to Bidder.

The MBA still has some of the postcards. The 400 or so that weren't returned had probably got lost. **18** ______ But somehow, the one carrying the recently returned postcard had remained in the sea for over a hundred years. It appears it finally found its way to a sandy beach on Amrum Island, just off the coast near the German-Danish border. **19** ______ After breaking the bottle open, she filled out the postcard and sent it off to the MBA, not realising she was posting a message from the distant past.

Unfortunately, the delayed arrival of Bidder's old postcard at the MBA offices hasn't added to what staff there already know about the North Sea currents. **20** ______ What happened in between remains a mystery!

A	It's also possible that the bottles containing them had broken.
B	However, they were never found.
C	They believe it shows how much marine science has changed.
D	Most of them were discovered within four years of this experiment.
E	On the other, were directions on how to mail it back.
F	All it tells them is where it was dropped and where it was found.
G	She worked with Bidder to understand how fish move through the oceans.
H	It was then picked up by a woman on holiday there.

Part 5

Questions 21–26

For each question, choose the correct answer.

Swordfish

Swordfish are a species of large fish. They live in the Indian, Atlantic and Pacific Oceans, and they are easy to recognise because of the **(21)** .... long, sharp point that grows out from the front of their heads.

Although they **(22)** .... to prefer warmer waters, they can live in quite a **(23)** .... range of temperatures. They travel to warmer waters in the winter and cooler ones in the summer.

Female swordfish are generally larger than the males of the species. The largest swordfish ever caught weighed 536 kilogrammes, and it is **(24)** .... that they can grow to be over 4 metres in length. They live for around 9 years.

Swordfish hunt other ocean fish. They are able to swim at **(25)** .... speed – up to an amazing 80 kilometres per hour. This gives them an important **(26)** .... over other sea creatures when they are searching for food.

21	**A**	definitely	**B**	extremely	**C**	totally	**D**	completely
22	**A**	look	**B**	think	**C**	choose	**D**	seem
23	**A**	wide	**B**	steep	**C**	high	**D**	deep
24	**A**	believed	**B**	appeared	**C**	decided	**D**	admitted
25	**A**	hard	**B**	large	**C**	great	**D**	strong
26	**A**	achievement	**B**	development	**C**	advantage	**D**	condition

Part 6

Questions 27–32

For each question, write the correct answer.
Write **one** word for each gap.

How to hold a fun party

Are you thinking about holding a party? Then you need to make sure it's lots of fun! Invite plenty **(27)** .... people and include a few surprises. For example, if you're serving food, try ordering ten pizzas **(28)** .... are the same flavour but come from different restaurants in your area. Then have a 'taste test' and vote on **(29)** .... best one. Or how **(30)** .... playing games? You could have a video games tournament and offer prizes for the winners. You could also have a singing competition and ask each guest to sing a song.

If your party includes a meal around a table, for each new course, ask your guests to sit next to someone different, in **(31)** .... to talk to as many different people **(32)** .... possible. Finally, play fun music: your guests might even get up and dance!

WRITING (45 minutes)

Part 1

You **must** answer this question.
Write your answer in about **100 words** on the answer sheet.

Question 1

Read this email from your English-speaking friend Jamie and the notes you have made.

EMAIL

From: Jamie

Subject: Your visit

Hi,

I'm so glad you're coming to visit me next weekend. — *Me too!*

The weather will be good and it would be nice to spend a whole day outdoors. We could go horse riding or take a boat trip on the river. What would you like to do? — *Tell Jamie*

I've invited some friends round for the evening while you're here. Each of my friends is going to bring something to eat. Could you make a dish too? — *Offer …*

Have you got any questions about your visit? — *Ask about transport to Jamie's house*

See you soon!

Jamie

Write your **email** to Jamie using **all the notes**.

Part 2

Choose **one** of these questions.
Write your answer in about **100 words** on the answer sheet.

Question 2

You see this announcement on an English-language website.

> **Articles wanted!**
>
> **A great film**
>
> What's your favourite film?
>
> What do you like about it?
>
> How important is it to read film reviews before choosing which film to see?
>
> Write an article answering these questions, and we'll publish the best ones on our website.

Write your **article**.

Question 3

Your English teacher has asked you to write a story.
Your story must begin with this sentence.

Jan was surprised when her friend gave her a large brown envelope.

Write your **story**.

LISTENING (approximately 30 minutes)

Part 1

Questions 1–7

For each question, choose the correct answer.

---

1 What has the man lost?

A

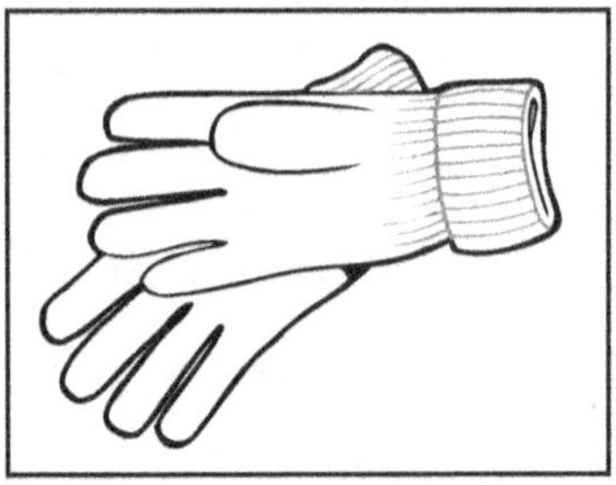

B

C

2 What is the woman going to do tomorrow?

A

B

C

3 Which items cost less than usual at the moment?

A

B

C

4 Which place will the people visit first on the tour?

A

B

C

5 Which tickets did the man buy?

A

B

C

6 What does the man want to buy?

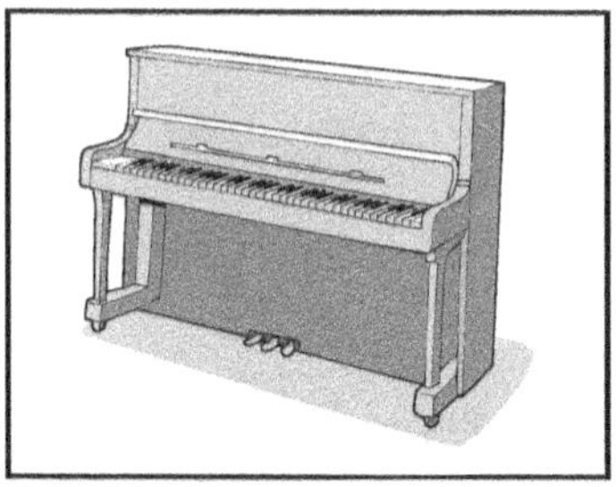

A

B

C

7 Which type of exercise does the doctor recommend?

A

B

C

Part 2

Questions 8–13

For each question, choose the correct answer.

---

8 You will hear two friends talking about a hotel.
They agree that

A the staff are very friendly.

B the rooms have good views.

C the food there is excellent.

9 You will hear two friends talking about an art exhibition.
Why was the woman disappointed with it?

A There weren't many paintings.

B It was very expensive.

C The gallery was too dark.

10 You will hear two friends talking about a book they've read.
They both think it would be better if it had

A a more original ending.

B more interesting characters.

C more action in the story.

11 You will hear a woman telling a friend about a visit to the hairdresser's.
What does she say about it?

A The haircut wasn't good value.

B The place wasn't very tidy.

C The hairdresser wasn't very friendly.

12 You will hear a woman telling a friend about her singing class.
What is she surprised about?

A the size of the group

B how confident she feels about singing

C the attention she gets from the teacher

13 You will hear two friends talking about a new sports centre.
What do they agree would improve it?

A reducing the entry price

B offering classes at different times

C changing the temperature in the pool

Part 3

Questions 14–19

For each question, write the correct answer in the gap.
Write **one** or **two words** or a **number** or a **date** or a **time**.

You will hear a guide giving information to people who are going to watch a car race involving old cars.

Classic car race

Before the race

- see the cars, next to the **(14)** ....
- enter a competition to win a **(15)** ....
- buy **(16)** .... at a lower price than usual at the café

The race

- starts at **(17)** .... p.m.

After the race

- use the **(18)** .... exit to get to the station
- upload your photos to **(19)** www.........................org

Part 4

Questions 20–25

For each question, choose the correct answer.

You will hear an interview with a young writer called Jenny Taylor, who has just had her first novel published.

20 What does Jenny say about school?

A She read a lot of poems there.
B She was proud of what she wrote there.
C She admired someone there.

21 How did Jenny get the idea for her first novel?

A talking to friends and family
B watching strangers
C looking on the internet

22 What's Jenny's novel about?

A a famous historical event
B a long journey
C a family's problems

23 How does Jenny feel about her novel?

A satisfied that it has a good story
B pleased that people are buying it
C surprised that it was published

24 What does Jenny say about her writing routine?

A She does her best writing in the morning.
B She wears pyjamas when she writes.
C She likes to write a similar amount every day.

25 What does Jenny usually read for pleasure?

A funny stories
B exciting stories
C true stories

Draft

OFFICE USE ONLY - DO NOT WRITE OR MAKE ANY MARK ABOVE THIS LINE Page 1 of 2

Cambridge Assessment English

Candidate Name		Candidate Number	
Centre Name		Centre Number	
Examination Title		Examination Details	
Candidate Signature		Assessment Date	

Supervisor: If the candidate is ABSENT or has WITHDRAWN shade here O

Preliminary Reading Candidate Answer Sheet

Instructions
Use a PENCIL (B or HB)
Rub out any answer you want to change with an eraser.

For Parts 1, 2, 3, 4 and 5:
Mark ONE letter for each answer.
For example: If you think A is the right answer to the question, mark your answer sheet like this:

0	A ●	B O	C O

Part 1

1	A O	B O	C O
2	A O	B O	C O
3	A O	B O	C O
4	A O	B O	C O
5	A O	B O	C O

Part 2

6	A O	B O	C O	D O	E O	F O	G O	H O
7	A O	B O	C O	D O	E O	F O	G O	H O
8	A O	B O	C O	D O	E O	F O	G O	H O
9	A O	B O	C O	D O	E O	F O	G O	H O
10	A O	B O	C O	D O	E O	F O	G O	H O

Part 3

11	A O	B O	C O	D O
12	A O	B O	C O	D O
13	A O	B O	C O	D O
14	A O	B O	C O	D O
15	A O	B O	C O	D O

Part 4

16	A O	B O	C O	D O	E O	F O	G O	H O
17	A O	B O	C O	D O	E O	F O	G O	H O
18	A O	B O	C O	D O	E O	F O	G O	H O
19	A O	B O	C O	D O	E O	F O	G O	H O
20	A O	B O	C O	D O	E O	F O	G O	H O

Part 5

21	A O	B O	C O	D O
22	A O	B O	C O	D O
23	A O	B O	C O	D O
24	A O	B O	C O	D O
25	A O	B O	C O	D O
26	A O	B O	C O	D O

Continues over ➡

OFFICE USE ONLY - DO NOT WRITE OR MAKE ANY MARK BELOW THIS LINE Page 1 of 2

Draft

Draft

OFFICE USE ONLY - DO NOT WRITE OR MAKE ANY MARK ABOVE THIS LINE

Page 2 of 2

For Part 6:
Write your answers clearly in the spaces next to the numbers (27 to 32) like this:

0 ENGLISH

Write your answers in CAPITAL LETTERS.

Part 6		Do not write below here
27		27 1 O 0 O
28		28 1 O 0 O
29		29 1 O 0 O
30		30 1 O 0 O
31		31 1 O 0 O
32		32 1 O 0 O

OFFICE USE ONLY - DO NOT WRITE OR MAKE ANY MARK BELOW THIS LINE

Page 2 of 2

Draft

You must write within the grey lines.

Write your answer for Part 1 below. Do not write on the barcodes.

Question 1

This section for use by Examiner only:

C	CA	O	L

* 0010437500302 *

You must write within the grey lines.

Answer only one of the two questions for Part 2.
Tick the box to show which question you have answered.
Write your answer below. Do not write on the barcodes.

Part 2	Question 2 ☐	Question 3 ☐

This section for use by Examiner only:

C	CA	O	L

* 0010437500303 *

Draft

OFFICE USE ONLY - DO NOT WRITE OR MAKE ANY MARK ABOVE THIS LINE

Page 1 of 1

Cambridge Assessment English

Candidate Name		Candidate Number	
Centre Name		Centre Number	
Examination Title		Examination Details	
Candidate Signature		Assessment Date	

Supervisor: If the candidate is ABSENT or has WITHDRAWN shade here ○

Preliminary Listening Candidate Answer Sheet

Instructions

Use a PENCIL (B or HB). Rub out any answer you want to change with an eraser.

For Parts 1, 2 and 4:
Mark one letter for each answer. For example: If you think **A** is the right answer to the question, mark your answer sheet like this:

0 A B C

For Part 3:
Write your answers clearly in the spaces next to the numbers (14 to 19) like this:

0 ENGLISH

Write your answers in CAPITAL LETTERS.

Part 1			
1	A ○	B ○	C ○
2	A ○	B ○	C ○
3	A ○	B ○	C ○
4	A ○	B ○	C ○
5	A ○	B ○	C ○
6	A ○	B ○	C ○
7	A ○	B ○	C ○

Part 2			
8	A ○	B ○	C ○
9	A ○	B ○	C ○
10	A ○	B ○	C ○
11	A ○	B ○	C ○
12	A ○	B ○	C ○
13	A ○	B ○	C ○

Part 3		Do not write below here
14		14 1 ○ 0 ○
15		15 1 ○ 0 ○
16		16 1 ○ 0 ○
17		17 1 ○ 0 ○
18		18 1 ○ 0 ○
19		19 1 ○ 0 ○

Part 4			
20	A ○	B ○	C ○
21	A ○	B ○	C ○
22	A ○	B ○	C ○
23	A ○	B ○	C ○
24	A ○	B ○	C ○
25	A ○	B ○	C ○

OFFICE USE ONLY - DO NOT WRITE OR MAKE ANY MARK BELOW THIS LINE

Page 1 of 1

Draft

Acknowledgements

The authors and publishers acknowledge the following sources of copyright material and are grateful for the permissions granted. While every effort has been made, it has not always been possible to identify the sources of all the material used, or to trace all copyright holders. If any omissions are brought to our notice, we will be happy to include the appropriate acknowledgements on reprinting and in the next update to the digital edition, as applicable.

Photographs

All the photographs are sourced from Getty Images.

Key: T = Test R = Reading; S = Speaking.

T1 R: Yagi Studio/DigitalVision; eurobanks/iStock/Getty Images Plus; Hero Images; David Schaffer/Caiaimage; **T2 R:** Hero Images; Wavebreakmedia/iStock/Getty Images Plus; SanneBerg/iStock/Getty Images Plus; Westend61; iStock/Getty Images Plus; **T3 R:** monkeybusinessimages/iStock/Getty Images Plus; Sam Edwards/OJO Images; Morsa Images/DigitalVision; Portra/E+; janetleerhodes/iStock/Getty Images Plus; **T4 R:** Westend61; Tony Anderson/DigitalVision; Alexander Spatari/Moment; Maskot; Caiaimage/Sam Edwards/Caiaimage; Jeff Rotman/Photolibrary; **T1 S:** Stanislaw Pytel/DigitalVision; Andersen RossPhotography Inc/DigitalVision; **T2 S:** Jacobs Stock Photography Ltd/DigitalVision; sot/DigitalVision; **T3 S:** Thomas Barwick/DigitalVision; Ultra.F/Photodisc; **T4 S:** JohnnyGreig/E+; Hero Images.

Illustrations commissioned by Cambridge Assessment.

Typeset by QBS Learning.

Audio production by Real Deal Productions and dsound recording.

Visual materials for the Speaking test

Test 1

Part 2

Task 1A

Task 1B

Test 1

Part 3

Task 1C

Learning about a new country

Test 2

Task 2A

Task 2B

Test 2

Part 3

Task 2C

Advertising

Test 3

Task 3A

Task 3B

Test 3

Part 3

Task 3C

Sightseeing in a city

Test 4

Task 4A

Task 4B

Test 4

Part 3

Task 4C

Learning a new skill

Caiaimage/Sam Edwards/Getty I